STEPNEY
THEN & NOW
IN COLOUR

SAMANTHA L. BIRD

The History Press

First published in 2013

The History Press
The Mill, Brimscombe Port
Stroud, Gloucestershire, GL5 2QG
www.thehistorypress.co.uk

British Library Cataloguing in Publication Data.
A catalogue record for this book is available from the British
Library.

ISBN 978 0 7524 7958 3

Typesetting and origination by The History Press
Printed in India.

CONTENTS

ACKNOWLEDGEMENTS

I would like to thank all those who have been involved in creating this book. To Michelle Tilling, my thanks for seeking me out on Twitter and commissioning this book. I would also like to thank all the staff at Tower Hamlets Local History Library and Archives, in particular Malcolm Barr-Hamilton, for all their help in making this book possible. Finally, my thanks go out to my husband, Hooch, for his total support in all my research, without which none of this would be possible. Hooch, you might actually look at the pictures in this book!

All original photographs, apart from the East End Mission Hall (pp. 48–9), are reproduced with the kind permission of Tower Hamlets Local History Library and Archives. The photograph of the East End Mission is reproduced by kind permission of the City of London, London Metropolitan Archives.

ABOUT THE AUTHOR

Dr Samantha L. Bird completed her PhD on Stepney borough in 2009. Since then she has had her thesis published by Cambridge Scholars Publishing – *Stepney: Profile of a London Borough from the Outbreak of the First World War to the Festival of Britain, 1914–1951*. She has also written numerous articles and most notably had an article published on the East End and the Blitz in the *BBC History Magazine*. She is constantly broadening her knowledge of Stepney and is currently looking at the papers of the late Denis Delay, a trade union leader, who was writing a book on the history of the docks when he died in April 2011.

INTRODUCTION

Stepney no longer exists and is now part of Tower Hamlets along with Bethnal Green and Poplar. To the north Stepney was bordered by Bethnal Green, to the east by Poplar, to the south by the River Thames and to the west by the City of London. The Metropolitan Borough of Stepney was established in 1899 by the London Government Act and included the parishes of Mile End Old Town, St George-in-the-East, the districts of Limehouse and the Whitechapel Boards of Works, including the Tower of London. It is the boundaries of the Metropolitan Borough of Stepney that I have used in this book, as the majority of the original pictures have come from the time of its existence.

Stepney is an area with many very well-known associations and images, from the horrifying murders of Jack the Ripper to the soaking up of the heavy bomb damage during the Blitz, from the classical confrontation between Mosley's fascists and the socialist left at the Battle of Cable Street to the dramatic Siege of Sidney Street when Liberal Home Secretary Winston Churchill rooted out an anarchist cell. It is only once all the pictures have been gathered together that one really appreciates what an intense and varied history Stepney has had.

Through the religious buildings depicted in this book, one can appreciate the variety of ethnic and religious groups who have lived in Stepney, from St Dunstan's, the original Anglican parish church, to the St George Lutheran Church, which is the oldest German Church in Britain. There's also the Protestant Chapel set up on Brick Lane by the French Huguenots which became Spitalfields Great Synagogue for the Jewish immigrants in the late nineteenth century and today is the Brick Lane Jamme Masjid (Brick Lane Great Mosque). These buildings reflect the evolution of the population in the borough of Stepney, an area which has always been seen as a part of the poor East End. Philanthropists saw Stepney and the East End as needing their help, hence, such companies as the Four Per Cent Dwelling Company built the Charlotte de Rothschild Buildings and many others. The Jewish Soup Kitchen was also set up by the wealthier Jewish people within the community to help the poorer members. There was also the building of almshouses for shipmasters or widows.

During the Second World War, Stepney suffered extensive destruction as within its boundaries there are many important positions: the docks, the hospital, the gas works and industry in general. With bombers aiming for these key targets, more widespread destruction of the borough occurred, which caused chaos for residents. I have included some pictures of the devastation caused by the air raids because for Stepney this was to be such a significant event in shaping the borough we see today.

Some of the key thoroughfares into the City of London from the east pass through Stepney with the A11 and A13 both cutting through the borough. Away from the main roads, Stepney has some beautiful areas with quiet neighbourhoods and green open spaces for people to enjoy. Today Stepney showcases a variety of buildings, which reflect the diversity of cultures that have lived and continue to live here.

TOWER OF LONDON

THE TOWER OF LONDON is perhaps the most well-known building in Stepney, although many would probably not realise that it was within the borough, it being at the most western point. This ancient place has been fortress, palace and prison; much of the darker history of England is associated with this range of buildings overlooking the River Thames, by which, in days gone by, it was most conveniently approached. The fortress itself dates from 1078. After William of Normandy conquered England in 1066, the White Tower was established in order to keep hostile Londoners at bay. The Tower buildings were added in succeeding reigns, and down to the time of Charles II, all the English sovereigns held their City abode at the Tower.

THE TOWER OF LONDON is one of the great attractions of the metropolis. Year in and year out, day by day, there is a steady stream of visitors. Whatever else may be omitted, the Tower of London must be visited before one can say they have seen the sights of London. It is estimated that over two million people visit it each year. With so much of England's history intertwined with the Tower, it is not surprising.

TOWER BEACH

TOWER BEACH, BY THE TOWER OF LONDON in 1937. People once bathed freely in the Thames, strange as it might seem today. From 1934 to 1939 and 1946 to 1971 the foreshore at the Tower was the site of the Tower of London Children's Beach, a much enjoyed and fondly remembered recreation of the seaside in Central London. The Children's Beach owed its existence to Lord Wakefield and the Vicar of All Hallows, the Revd P.B. Clayton. Some 50ft wide, and made from sand on gravel, there was room for 3,000 children at a time. The beach was opened under the auspices of the Tower Hill Improvement Trust in July 1936 in a grand ceremony attended by the Lord Mayor, the Bishop of London, the Lieutenant of the Tower and other dignitaries. King George V had been petitioned for permission to create the beach and replied through his Private Secretary that he was pleased to give his entire approval to the project that would, he felt, give a much needed and health giving playground to the children of the district.

TODAY THE BEACH IS CLOSED, and it is only with low tide that one can catch a glimpse of what it might have been like. The sand on gravel has all but been washed out to sea.

ENTRANCE TO ST KATHARINE'S DOCK

THE ENTRANCE TO ST KATHARINE'S DOCK, St Katharine's Way, 1960.
St Katharine's Dock is situated to the east of the Tower of London. When
the St Katharine's Dock Bill was passed in 1825, there were some 1,250 slum
houses which, along with St Katharine's hospital, were to be cleared to make
way for the ambitious centre for London's commerce and industry.
In 1852 Ivory House was built with its distinctive clock tower. St Katharine's
Dock had a reputation for handling valuable cargoes from Europe, the West
Indies, Africa and the Far East, such as sugar, tea, rum, spices, perfumes, ivory,
shells, marble, indigo, wine and brandy, and the docks thrived. By the 1930s
St Katharine's Dock was described as a focal point for the world's greatest
concentration of portable wealth. However, between the wars, world trade
ships became too large to dock here. During the Second World War,
St Katharine's Dock was used for war work and became a victim of the Blitz.

TODAY, THE VISIONS OF THE ORIGINAL DESIGNER, Thomas Telford, and architect, Philip Hardwick, to build six-storey warehouses with cast iron window frames and extensive vaults to store thousands of casks of valuable wine and other luxury goods can still be seen in the modern office blocks such as the International House and Commodity Quay. Both office blocks sympathetically mirror the architecture of the imposing warehouses which stood on the site before them. Ivory House with its distinctive clock tower today houses luxury warehouse apartments, and on the ground floor there are small restaurants and shops.

ENTRANCE TO THE LONDON DOCKS

ENTRANCE TO THE LONDON DOCKS, East Smithfield, *c.* 1969. The London Docks are approximately half a mile to the east of St Katharine's Dock, and the designer and architect were Daniel Asher Alexander and John Rennie. They were opened in 1805 and covered an area of about 90 acres, of which 35 acres consisted of water, and there was almost 2½ miles of quay and jetty frontage. The docks were surrounded by a high wall and had room for over 300 vessels. The warehouses were four storeys high and could hold over 200,000 tons of goods. In 1858 two new docks were constructed for larger vessels that could provide berths for vessels up to 3,000 tons gross register. Also, in 1850 the wool floors were enlarged and roofed with glass. These warehouses alone had over 40 acres of floor area.

THE LONDON DOCKS not only housed the goods unloading at the docks themselves, but a great quantity of goods from ocean-going vessels discharging lower down the river were brought up to the London and St Katharine's Docks by river lighters and road conveyances for storage. The entrance to the London Docks today is situated between The Highway and the Tower of London on one of the main thoroughfares into the City. As you can see, the entrance to the dock still exists. However, the docks are now mainly luxury apartments and office space.

ST GEORGE-IN-THE-EAST BATHS, BETTS STREET

ST GEORGE-IN-THE-EAST BATHS, Betts Street, north of The Highway, drawn in 1890. The first bath to open in London was in 1847, also in Stepney borough at Goulston Square, Whitechapel, with the Prince Consort laying the foundation stone. St George Bath was a second class swimming bath and was available during the summer season on Mondays, Wednesdays, Fridays and Saturdays for men. All day on Tuesdays and up to 4 p.m. on Thursdays the baths were open for women, and on Thursday evening and Sunday mornings, it was open for mixed bathing. There were also Slipper Baths for both sexes, first and second class, and a public washhouse which was well patronised and open every weekday except Bank Holidays. Alexander Gander remembered Mr Schmieden, the baker on Cable Street, who would give the young boys a stale cake or roll when they came out of Betts Street Baths after a swim or hot bath. A favourite schoolboy prank was to call the attendant for cold water for the cubicle that a friend was in. Children were sent to the baths for a weekly bath, so some amusement had to be found for this punishment! Betts Street became known as Tiger Bay, not because of Jamrach's animal emporium, where any species of wild animal could be bought or sold, but because of its 'Tigresses' or feisty prostitutes with startling clothes and colourful boots.

THE GOULSTON SQUARE WASH HOUSE, the first wash house to be opened in London, was demolished in 1989, and the site was reused to build the Women's Library in 2001, which still retains the front façade of the original wash house. The Betts Street Baths have disappeared completely. After the First World War, the London County Council built Betts House which consists of forty flats. Betts Street originally attached Cable Street to The Highway but today is a cul-de-sac with Betts House to the east of the street and Betts Street Playschool to the west. There are no longer the public baths, and the swimming pool has moved east along The Highway. Jamrach's animal emporium, which had a menagerie on Betts Street, struggled through the First World War, with Charles Jamrach's son Albert taking over the business. However, after the death of Albert in 1917, the firm went out of business in 1919.

WAINWRIGHT HOUSE, GARNET STREET

WAINWRIGHT HOUSE IS ON GARNET STREET, which is south of The Highway. The dwellings seen to the left in about 1950 are situated at the junction of New Gravel Lane and Prusom Street. Wainwright House was completed in August 1932 and was named after the late Father Lincoln Stanhope Wainwright, who lived and worked in this part of the borough for over fifty years. Wainwright came to Wapping in 1873 as a curate to his predecessor, Father C.F. Lowder. In serving the people, Wainwright was a living saint, working tirelessly for the people in the area, giving away the very clothes and shoes he wore. He once found a young lad trying to steal a clock from the clergy house but managed to persuade the lad to go to the kitchen for a cup of cocoa. He spoke to the lad at some length and soon he had the would-be thief serving mass in St Peter's and in employment. Wainwright died in February 1929 in St Peter's Clergy House and the people of Wapping stood in line to climb the uncarpeted stairs to view the mortal remains of one who had been their priest and friend for a lifetime.

TODAY, ON CLERGY HOUSE, Wapping Lane, which is the neighbouring street to the west of Garnet Street, there is a blue plaque dedicated to L.S. Wainwright. Wainwright House, Garnet Street, can accommodate up to sixty persons in twenty two-roomed flats and was opened in 1932 by the first female Mayor of Stepney, Miss Miriam Moses, and the plaque dedicating the event is clearly visible in the picture. Moses was a Liberal who followed her father into a life in the public arena and Jewish communal service. She was a member of the Whitechapel and Stepney Board of Guardians and in 1922 was to become the first female Justice of the Peace in Whitechapel. Moses and Elsie Cohen established the Brady Girl's Club at Buxton Street School in 1925, which Moses was involved in for most of her life. Moses was also vice-president of the Stepney Liberal Association. She has a blue plaque on 17 Princelet Street where she was born in 1886, which is to the west of Brick Lane.

ST GEORGE-IN-THE-EAST CHURCH

ST GEORGE-IN-THE-EAST CHURCH is sandwiched between Cable
Street to the north and The Highway to the south, and is seen here
in 1944. St George-in-the-East is an Anglican Church and one of
Nicholas Hawksmoor's six churches in London. It was built between
1714 and 1729 and funded by the 1711 Act of Parliament. The
churchyard holds tombstones recording the buried victims of the
murders in the Ratcliff Highway. The murders were two vicious
attacks on two separate families that resulted in multiple fatalities
which occurred over a twelve-day period in December 1811 in homes
that were only half a mile apart in the Wapping area. One John
Williams was declared the murderer after he committed suicide in
his prison cell on 28 December 1811. In 1859/60 the church was
famous due to the rectorship of the then famous Bryan King. King
took a leading part in the Anglo-Catholic movement of the day, and
it was his attempt to introduce ritualistic services in the church
that led to disorderly and riotous scenes. For a time these scenes
aroused national interest and feeling which eventually resulted in
parliamentary action.

DURING THE SECOND WORLD WAR, in May 1941, St George-in-the-East was hit by a bomb. The original interior was destroyed by fire, but the walls and the distinctive pepper-pot towers remained. In 1964 a new modern interior was constructed within the original walls. Today the church has an active congregation and is open to the public on a daily basis between 9.00 a.m. and 6.00 p.m. In January 2010 the 150th anniversary of the Ritualism Riots was celebrated with a visit from the Archbishop of Canterbury, Dr Rowan Williams.

ST GEORGE'S NATURE STUDY

ST GEORGE'S NATURE STUDY is within the grounds of St George-in-the-East's churchyard. The building dates from about 1877 when it served as a mortuary. However, in 1904 the rector, Harry Jones, converted the building into a museum: The Metropolitan Borough of Stepney Nature Museum. The museum was a branch of the Whitechapel Museum and was set up to teach slum dwellers something about nature as the children saw so little greenery around them. In the summer time, it has been suggested, that the museum often received 1,000 visitors per day, the majority being local school children. The museum had live exhibits such as reptiles, amphibians and tropical fish tanks. There were also stuffed animals and an array of butterflies. In the immediate surrounding area there was a wild flower garden with a beehive and an aviary. Several specimen trees were also planted in the garden when the museum was opened. Prior to the opening of the museum, Harry Jones had decided between 1874 and 1875 that the ragged churchyard attached to St George-in-the-East, which had been disused for burials for twenty years, and the graveyard at the back of the adjacent Wesleyan Chapel should be amalgamated into one and converted into a public garden for residents to enjoy.

IN 1939 THE MUSEUM was shut when the children in the area were evacuated out of London with the outbreak of the Second World War. This measure was seen as only temporary. However, the museum never reopened and fell into disrepair – today the windows and doors are filled with corrugated iron and the building is roofless. Above the doorway one can still make out the original sign: The Metropolitan Borough of Stepney Nature Study Museum. The gardens are still very busy today for the local community with people walking their dogs, children playing in the dedicated playground and people generally enjoying the green open space. It is a very pleasant cut-through between Cable Street, to the north, and The Highway, to the south. There is supposed to be a planned restoration project for the museum, which would, no doubt, once again be enjoyed by the local children.

WILTON'S MUSIC HALL

THE PHOTOGRAPH OF WILTON'S MUSIC HALL was taken in 1979, when the building was disused. Wilton's address is 1 Graces Alley, off Ensign Street which connects Cable Street to The Highway. John Wilton purchased the business in about 1850 – at that time it was a concert room built behind a pub that was licensed to put on full-length plays. Wilton enlarged the concert room three years later and replaced it with his 'Magnificent New Music Hall' in 1859. In thirty years Wilton's Music Hall had many of the best remembered acts of early popular entertainment perform there such as George Ware who wrote 'The Boy I love is up in the Gallery', and Arthur Lloyd and George Leybourne (Champagne Charlie), two of the first music hall stars to perform for royalty. By the end of the nineteenth century the East End was notorious for being poverty stricken and having terrible living conditions. Religious organisations tried to help, and in 1888 Wilton's was purchased by The East London Methodist Mission. The mission renamed it The Mahogany Bar Mission and in 1889, with the Great Dock Strike, opened up as a soup kitchen, feeding 1,000 starving dockers and their families each day. The mission was to stay open for seventy years through some of the most testing conditions such as the Battle of Cable Street in 1936, and the Blitz during the Second World War, and throughout this period they continued to help the community and in particular the children of the borough.

WILTON'S WAS TO SURVIVE the post-Second World War slum clearance programme, and in 1971 the building was given a grade II listing. By 1997 Wilton's reopened as a theatre and concert hall and in 2012 the SITA trust awarded the venue £700,000 to begin Phase 1 of their ongoing project. The grant along with funds already raised means that major work can be carried out on the roof, basement, soundproofing, ventilation and electrics, where it is most needed. This will be a key step to preserving the music hall for future generations. The music hall is used for a variety of performances: comedy, plays, drama, magic and music. The Mahogany Bar is a thriving bar these days, and Wilton's is building its reputation once more.

SIDNEY SQUARE

SIDNEY SQUARE IS AT THE HEART OF SIDNEY STREET, which connects Mile End Road to Commercial Road. The picture shows four nissen huts which were situated on the north side of the square. The nissen huts are a prefabricated steel structure made from a half-cylindrical skin of corrugated steel. At the end of the Second World War, the housing crisis in Stepney was acute; it was estimated in the local newspaper *East End News* that in April 1945 some 650 families had been bombed out of their homes, and another 840 families were inadequately housed and in urgent need of accommodation. The nissen huts were a short-term solution to aid the housing crisis and were not very popular with the public as homes because, well, they were huts and not houses – at the end of the war, having endured so much, the people wanted proper homes. Also, rectangular furniture did not fit into a curved-wall house very well, therefore, the actual usable space within the hut was much less than anticipated.

THE NISSEN HUTS HAVE ALL DISAPPEARED NOW. Sidney Square was originally developed in the 1820s on former fields and the central garden was for the benefit of the residents in the surrounding terraces. The garden had been purchased by the London County Council and opened to the public in 1904. The terraces on the north side were the only ones affected by the Second World War and the two-storey terraces on the east and west sides have survived from the 1820s. The Sidney Street Estate on either side of the square represents Stepney Borough Council's first attempts at post-Second World War reconstruction. The estate was part of a large scheme of redevelopment, covering an area of approximately 26.93 acres which extended to Mile End Road to the north, Commercial Road to the south, Jubilee Street to the east and Sidney Street to the west. The area was to provide 677 new dwellings, a shopping centre, a large civic centre, amenity buildings such as a nursery school, a playground and open spaces.

SIDNEY STREET

THE SIEGE OF SIDNEY STREET, 1911. On 3 January 1911 it was reported that two
of the suspects from the Houndsditch Murders had besieged 100 Sidney Street. The
Houndsditch Murders of December 1910 centred on the killing of three policemen by
East European immigrants which had occurred after a group of Lettish men attempted to
rob H.S. Harris the Jewellers. The robbers made so much noise drilling a tunnel through
from a neighbouring property, that neighbours notified the authorities. The police then
made a forceful entrance, which was to have disastrous consequences. Along with the
three policemen who were killed, one of the robbers also died. The nation mourned the
deaths of the three policemen and was also shocked by the evidence that anarchists from
Europe appeared to be invading
England. On that fateful day in
Sidney Street, two of the Lettish
men besieged 100 Sidney
Street. Winston Churchill, the
Home Secretary, went to Sidney
Street to observe the police
and army as the gun battle
ensued. The affair drew to a
close when the house caught
fire and began to burn down.
Afterwards, Churchill was
criticised for not bringing out
the men alive. This event has
been described as the biggest
hue-and-cry since the Jack
the Ripper murders in 1888.

SIDNEY STREET RUNS NORTH–
SOUTH between Whitechapel
Road and Commercial Road.
The house of the siege was one
of eight four-storey red brick
tenement houses which were built in 1900 by Charles Martin, landlord of the Blind
Beggar public house, Whitechapel Road. The buildings survived the Second World War
but Stepney Borough Council demolished them in the post-war period. In 1959 Wexford
House was built on the site of 100 Sidney Street. Today, Wexford House is a quiet block of
flats and any trace of the site of the siege has all but disappeared. However, further along
Sidney Street towards Commercial Road, there is a newer block of flats called Siege House,
once again referring back to the notoriety the street once had.

WHITECHAPEL HIGH STREET

WHITECHAPEL HIGH STREET at the junction with
Osborne Street, *c.* 1890. Whitechapel High Street connects
Aldgate High Street with Whitechapel Road. In ancient
times it was part of the Roman road from London to
Colchester and it was paved as early as the reign of
Henry VIII. Owing to the importance of the High Street
as a major thoroughfare out of London, the sides were
built up rapidly and included many coaching inns and
taverns. Osborne Street is the southern extension of Brick
Lane, which enters Whitechapel High Street at its western
end. The street was once a narrow continuation of Brick
Lane and was known as 'Dirty Lane', but in the 1770s
the lane was widened and paved. It was named after the
Osborn family of Chicksand Priory, Bedfordshire, who were
prominent landowners in the area.

TODAY WHITECHAPEL HIGH STREET is part of the A11 and still one of the main thoroughfares from Aldgate to Essex. On the left corner of Whitechapel High Street and Osborn Street is Khushbu, a traditional desi (home style) Indian curry house, where curry is made fresh and served from the display. To the right is Clifton, which is also an authentic Asian restaurant. These two restaurants provide a gateway to Brick Lane with its many curry houses. Next to Clifton's is no. 7 Whitechapel Road, which is a commercial property. There are offices, studios and workshops in the building, which are advertised as being in a trendy, urban, city-fringe location. The area today is thriving for small businesses. A good selling point is that it has easy access to the City and yet is outside the congestion zone, but also one can take advantage of the superior transportation links.

GARDINER'S CORNER

GARDINER'S CORNER IS PROBABLY THE BIGGEST JUNCTION in Stepney as it brings
together Whitechapel Road (A11), Commercial Road (A13), Leman Street, Aldgate High
Street, and Commercial Street. Named after the Scottish clothing store Gardiners, which
is the central building in the picture, the junction was laid out in the 1870s and became
known as 'the gateway to the East End'. Gardiners store specialised in military uniforms
and children's clothing. Gardiner's Corner also played a role in the famous Battle of
Cable Street in 1936 as it was used as a meeting place for anti-fascist protestors. It
was a very appropriate meeting place as, from this junction, the protestors could take
any avenue into the East End to block the march of Oswald Mosley and his black-shirt
supporters. The bustling scene below was photographed in 1959.

IN 1971, AFTER NEARLY 100 YEARS of trading, Gardiners store closed. The following year, the six-storey building was destroyed by fire and while over two hundred firemen fought to save the landmark store, the 130ft high clock tower came crashing down on the streets below. The building was not replaced and by the early 1980s the Greater London Council constructed a one-way system at Gardiner's Corner which has totally changed the character of the site, as can be seen in the picture above. Today, the site of Gardiners is cordoned off and derelict. With so much redevelopment happening all around the site, it is no doubt only a matter of time before it is redeveloped with offices, as the area is a hub of office space. Diagonally opposite the junction is a huge office block which is in the process of being constructed.

CABLE STREET

CABLE STREET, 1936. The old photographs depict the morning of the Battle of Cable Street, 4 October 1936. The police are standing around waiting to see how the day unfolds, ready to react to whatever situation arises. Further down the street, one can see the blockade has already been put in place by the anti-fascist demonstrators, who were led by the Communist Party and by Phil Piratin in particular. The demonstrators are gathered behind the barricade, which was erected towards the west end of this long street near the junction of Christian Street, ready for Oswald Mosley and the British Union of Fascists to march their way. The march slogan of the demonstrators was 'They Shall Not Pass', which was inspired by the Spanish Civil War. It was estimated that some 300,000 demonstrators turned out, and 10,000 police, including 4,000 on horseback, tried to clear the road to allow the march to proceed. In the end, after a number of running battles, Mosley agreed to abandon the march to prevent further bloodshed. The marchers were then diverted towards Hyde Park to disperse, while anti-fascists rioted with the police. In all, 150 demonstrators were arrested and approximately 175 people were injured, including police, women and children.

CABLE STREET TODAY appears to have been widened to incorporate an extra lane for cyclists. It is a quiet street now that has completely changed its appearance since 1936. During the Second World War Cable Street suffered severe bombing and during a particularly heavy raid, Dr Hannah Billig, who practised in the area, stayed and tended to casualties, operating and binding tourniquets, with bombs falling within 20 yards of her. Billig was awarded the George Medal for her courage and bravery. A blue plaque was erected in her honour at 198 Cable Street where she was locally known as 'The Angel of Cable Street'. Looking at this picture, to the left-hand side one can see the Docklands Light Railway line running above archways, which are used as lock-ups today for small businesses. Shadwell station is further east along Cable Street.

ST GEORGE'S VESTRY HALL

ST GEORGE'S VESTRY HALL, Cable Street, 1875. In 1855 the Metropolis Management Act created a new system of local government for London which consisted of parish vestries and district boards of works. In what would become Stepney borough, there was the Limehouse District, Mile End Old Town Vestry, Whitechapel District and St George-in-the-East vestry. The Metropolitan Board was the forerunner of the London County Council and was an act for the better local management of the metropolis. In St George-in-the-East, the vestry hall was built to the east of Cable Street in 1861. It was built of Portland Stone with an Italianate façade at a cost of £6,000 and reportedly had a handsome interior. In 1899 further local government reforms were introduced with the London Government Act, which replaced all the vestries across London with twenty-eight borough councils. The new Stepney Borough Council took over the building as a local town hall until a new one could be built.

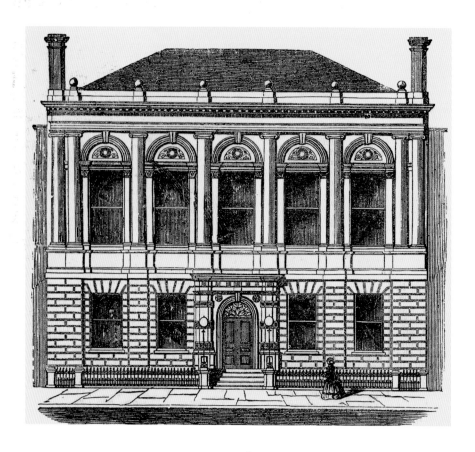

THE OLD TOWN HALL is today somewhat of a landmark due to the mural painted over the entirety of the west side of the building which depicts the Battle of Cable Street. The Tower Hamlets Arts Project commissioned the mural to commemorate the fiftieth anniversary of the battle and it was completed in the 1980s, although it suffered from acts of vandalism by anti-fascists before it was even finished. Dave Binnington, the original artist, was demoralised by this attack and retired from the project, the work being completed instead by Paul Butler, Desmond Rochford and Ray Walker, who each took a section. In 1985 and again in 1993 the mural was further damaged but was restored after the public appealed and was later treated with a protective coating. Since the creation of the London Borough of Tower Hamlets, which Stepney is engulfed by today, the building has been used by various offices and activities. Today it is a grade II listed building albeit in a somewhat dilapidated state.

CHRISTIAN STREET

CHRISTIAN STREET, TO THE EAST of Ellen Street, 1938. The first Zeppelin raid on London came on 31 May 1915. The German Commander Captain Linnarz in LZ18 found the blackout to be so ineffectual that he had little difficulty in spotting Commercial Road and from there headed for the docks. Stepney, on that first raid, was to take fifteen direct hits. The first bombs were dropped in the immediate vicinity of the Great Eastern Railway and Bishopsgate station and the last bomb, it was believed, was dropped in Duckett Street, near the Commercial Gas Works. Christian Street was hit twice with explosive bombs, and they were to cause the most injuries of the raid. Twelve people, all of whom were in the street at the time, were injured, and there was one fatality: Samuel Reuben, ten years old. By the time of this picture all evidence of the raid has disappeared and the street appears to be full of housing apart from the corner shop, Felds, which boasts of having salt beef and a delicatessen. In the windows above the shop dining rooms are advertised.

AFTER THE SECOND WORLD WAR, Christian Street was part of the London County Council housing scheme development, Berner Estate. For Christian Street alone this covered an area of 4.82 acres and was to comprise some 202 dwellings. Felds corner shop and the small houses have now been replaced by Danvers House and beyond it can be seen Hogarth Court. On the opposite side of the road to Danvers House and Ellen Street is Ropewalk Gardens. In 1999 a community garden was established on the Berner Estate, which was created by the Wapping Women's Centre. The garden was set up on a piece of disused land opposite Kindersley House, Pinchin Street, which is to the south of Christian Street. Many residents in the area had been growing vegetables on their balconies and the gardens have brought the women of the community together.

ELLEN STREET

ELLEN STREET RUNS PARALLEL to Cable Street between Christian Street to the east and Back Church Lane to the west, and is seen here in 1938. In the early 1920s the Stepney Housing Committee estimated that 36,217 houses were occupied by some 56,949 families or separate occupants. This gave the average persons per house as 7.7. The housing committee singled out particular areas for scrutiny, and Ellen Street was one of them. With an area of approximately 1¼ acres it included some 112 run-down houses for a population of 560. This meant that the number of persons per acre was 448, and for Stepney that was more than three times the census average for the borough of 141 persons per acre. It, therefore, showed that there were pockets of extreme overcrowding within the borough of Stepney. For example, in one five-roomed cottage, situated in an alley, two rooms were let by the tenant and in the remaining rooms the tenant, his wife and eight children, the eldest of which was fifteen, together with a lad of seventeen, who was the tenant's brother-in-law, all lived. By the time of this picture overcrowding and poor conditions were still a great issue. In Ellen House, Splidt Street, going south from Ellen Street, there were four flats on each landing but only two of the flats had a water closet and scullery, thus forcing the tenants to share necessities with the other two flats. This meant that the tenant who had the facilities had no privacy and arrangements had to be made so as not to overlap. Also, the staircases in the blocks were ill-lit and infested with vermin.

ELLEN STREET TODAY is a quiet street with fifty-nine homes on it, which are flats, maisonettes or apartments. The London County Council began rebuilding the area before the Second World War with the construction of Everard House on the opposite side of the road to this picture, between 1934 and 1936. Everard House is a long five-storey range with just a few private balconies. On the top floor originally were laundry rooms, but these were converted into flats in 1958/9. After the Second World War Hadfield House was constructed on the south side of Ellen Street in 1949. To the east a new approach to Ellen Street was introduced by Halliday House in 1961/2, which is an eight-storey block of flats with angled balconies.

PRESCOT STREET

PRESCOT STREET IS BORDERED to the west by Mansell Street and to the east by Leman Street, and it appears to have been one of the first streets in which the houses were distinguished by numbers instead of signs (Hatton's description of the street in 1708 notes the numbering). The street gained its name from its builder, Mr Prescot. In May 1741, the London Infirmary 'for the sick and diseased manufacturers, the seamen in the merchant service and their wives and families', moved from Featherstone Street, Moorfields, to Prescot Street. To begin with, a single house, no. 21, was rented from the executors of the late Sir William Leman at 24 guineas per year. With Prescot Street lying just outside the City of London's boundaries, the area was considered to have a very bad reputation. It had a number of brothels, disorderly taverns and theatres, such as the notorious Goodman's Fields New Wells Theatre, which was opened in 1703. By 1758, the London Infirmary had moved to Mount Field, Whitechapel Road, and the Magdalen Hospital, which provided a safe, desirable, and happy retreat for women and girls of the street, took over the site. In about 1888 the Princess of Prussia public house was built. It was named after Princess Anna Amelia (1723–87), a gifted musician whose sister married the Crown Prince of Prussia. Nos 1–9 were developed in art deco style between 1930 and 1933 by the Co-operative Wholesale Society (CWS) architect L.G. Ekins and were used by the Co-operative Bank. In the distance of this 1935 picture, one can see the striking clock tower of the grand headquarters of the CWS, built in 1887 on the corner of Leman Street and Hooper Street to the east of Prescot Street. It is a seven-storey structure in brick, granite and Portland stone and incorporates a sugar warehouse. The clock tower was designed by J.F. Goodey, a CWS committee member.

IN MORE RECENT TIMES the north side of Prescot Street has been the site of an archaeological project. Between March and October 2008 Prescot Street was an excavation site as it lies close to the centre of what is known as the East London Roman Cemetery in Aldgate, near to the City of London. It was hoped that the articles uncovered at this particular site would be able to give some insight to the archaeology of the Roman period and give some starting point for an exploration of Roman ideas about death and burial. There is also some evidence of medieval activity with some amazingly well-preserved leather on the site. Since that time the site has been transformed from an essentially rural area on the fringe of the City to a densely populated city centre district. After the excavation project, the new Grange Tower Bridge Hotel was built on the site, which can be seen in the picture. The hotel, opened in 2011, redefines luxury accommodation and event facilities within the Tower Bridge district. The Grange is one of the most energy efficient hotels to have opened in recent years with its renewable solar and photovoltaic panels and has an onsite borehole to reduce water consumption. Today the clock tower on the CWS building is still clearly visible at the east end of Prescot Street. The CWS headquarters, 99 Leman Street, known as the Sugar House, has been converted into luxury apartments.

ST GEORGE'S LUTHERAN CHURCH

ST GEORGE'S LUTHERAN CHURCH, Alie Street, *c.* 1920. The church was founded in 1762 and up until 1996 was used by the German Lutherans. St George's was the fifth Lutheran church to be built in London. The founder was Dietrich Beckman, a wealthy sugar refiner, and it was Beckman's cousin, Gustav Anton Wachsel who became the first pastor. Sugar refiners of German descent dominated the local area in the nineteenth century and, therefore, constituted the majority of the congregation. By 1853 the churchyard and crypt were closed. At its height approximately 16,000 German Lutherans resided in Whitechapel. Hanging in the church are the coat of arms of King George III and two carved timber commandment boards in German. The Royal Arms were required to be erected in Anglican churches, and this tradition was adopted by other churches as a mark of loyalty.

AFTER 1996 THE LUTHERAN CHURCH became the headquarters of the Historic Chapels Trust. The church is also still used for organ recitals. The organ was built in 1886 by the Walcker family, famous for organ building. They used the organ case of the previous organ by John England, 1794, and when the organ was rebuilt in 1937, the case was once again reused. Today, the church is the oldest surviving German Lutheran church in the United Kingdom. It still retains much of the original furnishings such as a complete set of pews and a high central double-decker pulpit and sounding board.

COMMERCIAL ROAD AND ADLER STREET

COMMERCIAL ROAD AND, TO THE NORTH, ADLER STREET, 1941.
As you can see from the picture, Adler Street was severely damaged
during the war with V1 bombs striking the area. The V1 bombs would
explode on the surface and cause a ripple effect of destruction. However,
in the middle of all the destruction stood the Morrison Building, which
was virtually unscathed. The Morrison Building was built in 1874
by the Improved Industrial Dwelling Company, which was founded in
1863 by Sir Sidney Waterlow. The company operated predominantly
in Central London providing block dwellings for the working classes.
They employed a strict selection and discipline regime among its
tenants, which ensured a healthy return on the investment and made
the company one of the more successful ones. At the height of the
company's success, it housed some 30,000 individuals.

THE MORRISON BUILDING still stands today. It is now engulfed by the Dryden Building to the east of Adler Street. The Dryden Building is a property of flats, like the Morrison Building. As one of the few large buildings which survived the Second World War, the Morrison Building is a good example of nineteenth-century architecture. The façade of the original building remains; however, the inside of the building has been modernised and extended to the rear in traditional form and upwards from roof level in a contemporary form. The buildings are situated in close proximity to Aldgate and Aldgate East station, the A11 Commercial Road and A13 Whitechapel Road plus an extensive bus service, taking one either into or out of the City.

CHRIST CHURCH, WATNEY STREET

CHRIST CHURCH, WATNEY STREET, which connects Commercial Road to Cable Street to the south, 1943. In 1838 a local builder, George Bridger, offered the Church Building Commissioner (CBC) the site of three houses on Watney Street, which he held on lease from the Mercers' Company. Bridger was willing to make a gift of the leaseholds, pay the Mercers for the freehold and compensate the tenants on three conditions. Firstly, it should be designed by John Shaw Junior. Secondly, the church should be built by Bridger and, finally, there should be no burial ground. The CBC agreed and the site was conveyed to them on 27 March 1839. Shaw designed Christ Church in the 'Lombardic' Romanesque (or Round) style. It was built in grey brick with stone dressing and slated pyramid spires on the two west end towers. The foundation stone was laid on 11 March 1840 and in 1845 two adjacent houses were adapted to provide a vicarage. William Quekett and his family lived in the vicarage, although he continued to curate at St George-in-the-East as well as Christ Church. Quekett actually worked on many projects while in the area. For instance in 1842 he instituted a Penny Savings Bank in Christ Church School, which in 1890 became part of the Post Office Savings Bank. He also helped to create the St Mary's Schools and St Mary's Church, Johnson Street. Quekett also took up the cause of 'distressed needlewomen' as well as setting up a lending library and reading room.

THE CHURCH AND THE VICARAGE were wrecked by a landmine on 16 April 1941 and the congregation was forced to move to St George-in-the-East. The ruins of the site stood for some years as seen in the photograph opposite, top, which was taken in 1943, before they were demolished. In 1952 the Archdeacon sent the Rector an 1839 shilling found under the foundation stone of Christ Church during its demolition. The Archdeacon commented 'I am sorry that we were not able to unearth something more substantial in the way of treasure.' The coin remains in the archives.

EAST END MISSION

THE EAST END MISSION, Commercial Road, 1957. The East End Mission was established in 1885 under the aegis of the Wesleyan Methodist Church. There were six centres in the borough of Stepney and one in the adjacent borough of Bethnal Green. Apart from the normal Sunday services there were thousands of weekday meetings of various kinds held during the year in connection with the programme of religious, social and philanthropic work conducted by the mission. The work was begun by Reverend Peter Thompson and by the late 1950s the mission employed seven ministers, one lay evangelist, seventeen deaconesses, five doctors, two nurses and dispensers in connection with the mission's surgeries, which dealt with about 2,500 people every week. Young people attended bible classes, youth clubs, Scouts and Guides, etc., and young parents had clubs where Christian responsibility was pointed out. There were also meetings for men, both young and old. The mission also had two out-reaches at Lambourne End and Ferrier Memorial Home, Westcliff-on-Sea, both in Essex. Despite receiving a small grant from the Methodist Mission headquarters, the East End Mission depended almost entirely upon voluntary contributions. They printed and published a monthly newspaper, *East End Star*. Throughout the mission's statement was that it existed to serve the people, to help in the making of good citizens, and to spread the Christian Gospel.

IN RECENT TIMES the East End Mission has been transformed with a mixture of new building work and refurbishments, comprising 100 apartments and commercial space. Out of 100 apartments, 81 private apartments were pre-sold to an investor and the remaining 19 were sold to One Housing Group for shared ownership. The redevelopment of the building was completed ahead of schedule in August 2008. The East End Mission received a Highly Commended award for Best Conversion Category as part of the Daily Telegraph, Your New Homes Awards, in March 2009.

LADY JANE MICO'S ALMSHOUSE

LADY JANE MICO'S ALMSHOUSE, Whitehorse Road, *c.* 1920. In 1670 Lady Jane Mico, the wife of Sir Samuel Mico, an alderman and mercer who died in 1666, bequeathed £1,500 to the Mercers' Company for the purpose of housing ten poor widows of London, who were fifty or older. The Mercers' Company took this to mean widows of Freemen of the City of London. However, due to a lack of funds the cottages were not built until 1691. In 1854 the company decided to rebuild the almshouses, and the current buildings were erected in 1856. As you can see, along the front of the cottages there are communal gardens, which are separated from the roadway by nineteenth-century railings and lime trees. At the rear of the cottages are small private gardens.

TODAY THE COTTAGES SITUATED BESIDE ST DUNSTAN'S CHURCHYARD are in a quiet, picturesque, part of Stepney. During the Second World War the almshouses suffered bomb damage and three houses were destroyed. In 1951 numbers 7 to 10 were rebuilt and a communal bathroom was added in the backyard for all ten cottages. The company wanted to make further improvements to the cottages in 1965, but the Greater London Council (GLC) would not permit the improvements as they had plans to increase public open spaces. Instead, new almshouses were built in Stepney. The Mercers' Company was offered a new site on the corner of Aylward Street and West Arbour Street. The new almshouses were built by the GLC on behalf of the Mercers' Company. Once the new ones were built, the GLC would take over the old almshouses in part exchange. Since the 1970s the almshouses have been private dwellings.

ST DUNSTAN'S CHURCH

ST DUNSTAN'S CHURCH, STEPNEY GREEN, 1890. The earliest record states that
St Dunstan rebuilt the church in 952. Although there have been many restorations and
the present building mainly dates from the fourteenth century, there are still examples of
the original Saxon work such as the rood near the organ and the corbel at the west end
in addition to a Norman window dating from the eleventh century. In 1901 there was a
fire in the church which destroyed the roof, altar, organ and vestries.

AFTER THE RESTORATION at a cost of over £7,000 the church was reopened in June 1902 by the Bishop of Stepney, Cosmo Gordon Lang, who became Archbishop of Canterbury. The ten bells at St Dunstan's were cast at the local Whitechapel Bell Foundry and are mentioned in the nursery rhyme 'Oranges and Lemons' – 'When will that be, say the bells of Stepney'. The church is surrounded by a churchyard of nearly 7 acres as during the Great Plague of London the churchyard was enlarged to cope with the massive number of deaths. In an eighteen-month period 6,583 died, and on one day in September 1665, no fewer than 154 people were buried. St Dunstan's still honours the fact that it was a sailor's church and the red ensign, the flag of the merchant navy, can often be seen flying from the flagpole. Historically, a light was used in the tower to guide ships to the port of London. Today, St Dunstan's is an active church and is open to visitors and worshippers from all over the world. There is also a close association between the church and two local schools: Stepney Greencoat Church of England Primary School and Sir John Cass and Redcoat Church of England Secondary School.

KING JOHN'S PALACE

KING JOHN'S PALACE on the corner of Garden Street and Stepney Green. On Gascoyne's map of 1703 the building is called King John's Court, but on early nineteenth-century maps the decayed mansion is called King John's Palace. The archway, which exists today, was the entrance to College Chapel, which was opened in 1831 by Stepney College and trained Baptist ministers from about 1811 to 1856. The college occupied several buildings to the east of the chapel, the oldest being a brick gatehouse. Between 1858 and 1859 most of the college buildings were demolished for two rows of houses on either side of the entrance to a new street named King John Street, which is now closed.

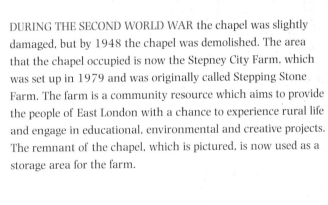

DURING THE SECOND WORLD WAR the chapel was slightly damaged, but by 1948 the chapel was demolished. The area that the chapel occupied is now the Stepney City Farm, which was set up in 1979 and was originally called Stepping Stone Farm. The farm is a community resource which aims to provide the people of East London with a chance to experience rural life and engage in educational, environmental and creative projects. The remnant of the chapel, which is pictured, is now used as a storage area for the farm.

THE RESIDENCE OF CAPTAIN COOK

RESIDENCE OF CAPTAIN COOK, 88 Mile End Road, *c.* 1910. The commemorative blue plaque high up on the wall of the house denotes the site where Captain James Cook (1728–79) used to live. Cook probably chose to live here as it was within easy walking distance of the River Thames yet still in semi-rural surroundings. The Royal Navy sent Cook on voyages of exploration and surveying that literally took him around the world. He surveyed the St Lawrence River in 1759, and in three voyages between 1768 and 1799 he charted the coasts of New Zealand, the East Coast of Australia, and the Pacific coast of North America. He was eventually killed by natives in Hawaii while trying to recover a ship they had stolen.

DESPITE THE BUILDING'S HISTORICAL SIGNIFICANCE, the residence of Captain Cook was allowed to be demolished in the 1960s to improve access to other premises at the rear of the building. Today, instead of the round blue plaque that was on the front of the house, a large commemorative inscription is set into the brick wall. The plaque was erected to commemorate the bicentenary of Cook's landing at Botany Bay, New South Wales, in April 1770.

THE METHODIST LYCETT CHAPEL

THE METHODIST LYCETT CHAPEL, Mile End Road, 1920s. The chapel stood on the corner of Mile End Road and Whitehorse Lane and was opened in 1881 as part of the Wesleyan East End Mission. It was named after Sir F. Lycett, who had taken great interest in the work of the Methodists in the East End. During the First World War, the chapel had one of the first National Kitchens in the country where people could obtain cheap, wholesome food. The facility was opened by Mrs Lloyd George, wife of the prime minister, in 1917. For local people it was 'the pictures' that pulled in the crowds as the chapel had realised that the slide shows and then moving images could enhance their ability to communicate their message to the wider community. The Methodist Lycett Chapel was at the forefront in the development of the cinema, and the chapel could seat 500 picturegoers. In the 1930s the Lycett had a major refurbishment, but then during the Second World War it suffered bomb damage and it was not until 1954 that the repairs were carried out. In the post-war years, a drop in population and therefore in the congregation along with a lack of staff led to the decision to close the Lycett Chapel in 1962.

AFTER THE CLOSURE of the Methodist Lycett Chapel, it was used as a warehouse, but in 1971 it was demolished. Today, Mile End Road is a busy thoroughfare into the City of London and the site of the chapel now has modern housing on it, as you can see from the picture.

THE LYCETT
The PEOPLE'S CHURCH
MEN
PLOUGH FIELDS AND SCATTER SEEDS
GOD
sends
SUN RAIN AND HARVEST
SMALL LEAKS
BIG SHIPS
LITTLE SINS
GREAT LIVES
THIS CHAPEL HAS BEEN
CONDEMNED
BUT NOT TO DIE
WATCH
NEW

REGENT'S CANAL BRIDGE

REGENT'S CANAL BRIDGE, Mile End Road, 1900. The Regent's Canal is 8.6 miles long and was dug by navvies between 1812 and 1820. It begins in Paddington and falls 96ft through twelve locks to the Regent's Canal Dock on the River Thames. Although a short canal, it was vital to London's docks as it provided the link to all the canals and navigable rivers in England. It was named after the Prince Regent, who became George IV in 1820. The main trade on the canal was coal, which was unloaded from colliers in the dock onto coal barges. The barges supplied coal merchants and several gas works along the canal, such as the Stepney Gas Works. There were a number of abortive attempts to convert the route of the canal into a railway line, but all of them failed due to either protests against the proposals or a lack of funds. After some years of negotiations, the canal was sold to the Regent's Canal and City Docks Railway Company for nearly £1.2 million in 1883. This time, instead of trying to build a railway, the company raised money for dock and canal improvement. In the twentieth century a new carrying subsidiary was formed, the Grand Union Canal Carrying Co., boasting a fleet of 186 pairs of narrow boats, which implemented a vigorous expansion policy and successfully drove new traffic along the canal. However, after the Second World War decline set in and the canal's commercial use was dwindling. By the late 1960s commercial vessels had almost ceased to operate as road haulage was taking the traffic that had not already been lost to the railways.

IN 1979 A NEW PURPOSE was found for the canal route when the Central Electricity Generating Board (CEGB) installed underground cables in a trough below the towpath between St John's Wood and City Road. These cables now form part of the National Grid supplying electrical power to London. Pumped canal water is circulated around the cables to act as a coolant while the canal itself is frequently used for pleasure cruising. Also, with increased environmental awareness, the towpaths along the canal have become a busy cycle route for commuters.

CHURCH OF THE GUARDIAN ANGELS

CHURCH OF THE GUARDIAN ANGELS, Mile End Road, 1903. The first Guardian Angels Catholic Church was opened on the Feast of the Immaculate Conception, 9 December 1868. It was originally on the site of a Congregationalist Church called the Salem Church whose pastor was a Mr Adams. Much to the surprise of Mr Adams, when the church could not raise the funds to purchase the church and the land, the landlord looked for a buyer elsewhere. A wealthy man called Charles Walker bought it as well as purchasing many other Catholic Church sites across London. It was only after 1791 when the Penal Laws changed that Catholic Mass could take place in England. After this time Catholic Missions began to be opened in the East End.

IN THE 1900s the original church building was condemned by the local council because the external walls were bulging and threatening to fall down on the congregation. The decision was made to knock down the old church and build a new one on the existing site. However, there was no money in the bank and none forthcoming from the diocese or the Archbishop, so the parish priest, Father Donleavy, turned to prayer. Approximately £6,000 was required and Lady Mary Howard answered the church's prayers by sending a cheque for £8,000 to build the new church in the memory of her sister. The architect Mr Frederick A. Walters was commissioned to design the church which was opened on another Marian Feast, the Feast of the Annunciation on Wednesday, 25 March 1903. It was opened by Bishop Bridle who travelled down to Stepney from Nottingham.

ST BENET'S CHURCH

ST BENET'S CHURCH, Mile End Road, *c.* 1907. The church was consecrated in 1872, but in 1940 St Benet's was bombed. The building was so named from having been built and endowed out of funds derived from the sale of St Benet's Church in Gracechurch Street in the City of London. St Benedict strove to live a simple life with a balance between physical work, intellectual study and prayer and, therefore, was an appropriate saint for the church's current association with Queen Mary College, University of London.

AFTER THE SECOND WORLD WAR, a new gault brick St Benet's was erected. The new St Benet's is a windowless block abutting a domed circular chapel with a hexagonal corona above the roof light. The new chapel was built in 1962/3 by Playne & Lacey & Partners. Today, St Benet's is incorporated into Queen Mary's College site.

THE PEOPLE'S PALACE

THE PEOPLE'S PALACE, Mile End Road *c.* 1905.
The novelist Sir Walter Besant paints a delightful picture
of a palace for the people in *All Sorts and Conditions of
Men.* In 1841 Mr J.T. Barber Beaumont bequeathed
the sum of £13,000 to provide, as he himself put it,
'intellectual improvement and rational recreation and
amusement for people living at the East End of London'.
A public movement raised a further £75,000 and the
Drapers' Company gave £20,000 for the purpose of a
technical school as well as selling the Beaumont Trustees
the site of the Bancroft Almshouses, upon which the
palace was erected. The original palace buildings were
designed by Mr E.R. Robson and had both recreation and
entertainment considered, with the large Queen's Hall, the
gardens, the library, club rooms, the clock tower and the
later added small hall, winter garden and swimming bath.
The Queen's Hall was named by Queen Victoria, and she
opened the building on 14 May 1887.

ON 25 FEBRUARY 1931 the People's Palace was destroyed by fire, but once again the Drapers' Company was to provide the finances to rebuild the technical college and create Queen Mary College in December 1934. A new People's Palace was constructed in St Helen's Terrace by the Metropolitan Borough of Stepney and was opened on 12 December 1936. Today the building is part of the Mile End Campus of Queen Mary College, which is home to the faculties of Humanities and Social Sciences, and Science and Engineering.

CHARRINGTONS BREWERY, MILE END ROAD

THE BREWERY HAD ORIGINALLY STARTED in Bethnal Green, but in 1757 Robert Westfield went into partnership with Joseph Moss and moved to new premises at Anchor Brewery, Mile End Road. By 1766 John Charrington took a third share in the business, which then traded as Westfield, Moss & Charrington. In 1769 Westfield retired, and Charrington purchased his share of the partnership. This was followed in 1783 by Moss retiring, leaving Joseph and his brother, Henry Charrington, in full control of the business. At the beginning of the nineteenth century, Charringtons was the second largest brewers in London. The brewery continued to be run by the Charrington family.

BY 1997 BASS AND CHARRINGTON sold off its public houses, and the buyer then created Punch Taverns. In 2000 the company sold off its brands to Interbrew, and its properties were sold to Six Continent Plc. Today the Charrington buildings have all but gone. Two of the gate posts remain, but the building has been lowered and now houses a retail park. The retail park is called Anchor Retail Park, which takes its name from the original Anchor Brewery that was on the premises. The building to the east is still the same and today is home to a firm of solicitors.

WICKHAMS DEPARTMENT STORE

WICKHAMS DEPARTMENT STORE, Mile End Road, designed by T. Jay Evans. The East End's major department store, on the north side of Mile End Road, was completed in 1927. In the early 1900s when the old row of shops were being acquired to build the store, the three Spiegelhalter brothers who operated a jewellers at no. 81 refused to part with their premises at any price. The Spiegelhalter family, of German descent, had lived at no. 81 for many years with most of their brothers and sisters being born there. The brothers' refusal to sell their premises led to the odd situation in which the new store was built around the family shop which continued to trade when Wickhams opened on both sides. The two parts of Wickhams form part of a greater design, as it was anticipated that the jewellers would eventually be purchased and incorporated into the building. Interestingly, if the building had been completed then the central column would have been offset, as there would have been seven windows to the west and nine to the east. It is as if the east wing of the building has been shifted over by the width of Spiegelhalter's shop.

THE GRAND DESIGN WAS NEVER COMPLETED, as can be seen from the modern view of the building, and it was Spiegelhalter's who had the last laugh. When the independent department store waned in the 1960s, the jewellers continued, and it was not until 1988 that the jewellers changed hands and became an off-licence. Today Tesco occupies much of the west wing and the east wing is home to Sports Direct. So, today two great chain stores are housed within what was once a great independent department store.

TRINITY ALMSHOUSES, MILE END ROAD

TRINITY ALMSHOUSES, MILE END ROAD, *c.* 1917. On the north side of Mile End Road was Trinity Green, which was to house the Trinity Hospital (Almshouses). The almshouses were erected in 1696 on land given for the purpose by Captain Henry Mudd of Ratcliff, Elder Brother of Trinity House, and endowed in 1701 by Captain Robert Sandes for twenty-eight masters of ships or their widows. The architect was Sir William Ogbourne. There are two rows of fourteen cottages, each with three rooms stacked on top of each other. They are facing a central courtyard and a separate chapel at the north end was included which dominates and provides spiritual navigation. The cottages are very structured but are enlivened with lyrical flourishes, such as the elaborately carved corbels above the doors, the model boats and stone balls topping off the edifice, and luxuriant stone crests adorning the brickwork. A tall mast stood at

the centre of the green during the nineteenth century to complete the look of a ship upon dry land. This was also emphasised by the concave walls at the front in place of a hull and the raised chapel at the aft where the poop deck would be. The almshouses were only a mile away from the docks, so it was a perfect spot for masters and commanders to enjoy their remaining years.

DURING THE SECOND WORLD WAR, the almshouses were bombed with the loss of the chapel and the rear eight cottages. After the conflict the red-brick cottages were modernised by the London County Council and today there is an atmosphere of repose in this small enclave, which is protected from the pandemonium of the Mile End Road and the A11 thoroughfare out of London to Essex by trees and green lawns. The cottages today are a mixture of public and private dwellings. In 2010, Dutch designer Eelke Jan Bles managed to purchase 5 Trinity Green and hired architect Chris Dyson to restore the building sympathetically and yet incorporate modern amenities. For any lucky visitor to 5 Trinity Green, they will gain a vision of how the whole place used to be.

THE LONDON HOSPITAL

THE LONDON HOSPITAL, Whitechapel Road, *c.* 1910. The London Hospital was originally named the London Infirmary and was founded in September 1740, the name changing in 1748. In November 1740, the first patients were treated at a house in Featherstone Street, Moorfields, and then the hospital moved to Prescot Street, Stepney, remaining there until 1757, when it moved once more to Whitechapel Road. Joseph Merrick, otherwise known as 'the Elephant Man', famously went to live at the London Hospital. Merrick travelled to London and was exhibited in a penny gaff shop on Whitechapel Road, which was rented by a showman Tom Norman. The shop, opposite the hospital, was visited by surgeon Frederick Treves, who invited Merrick to be examined and photographed. Soon after Norman's shop closed, Merrick was sent on tour in Europe but eventually made his way back to London. Unable to communicate, he was found by police to have Frederick Treves' card on his person and the surgeon agreed to take him back to the hospital. Although Merrick's condition was incurable, he was allowed to stay at the hospital for the remainder of his life and he and Treves developed a close friendship. Merrick also received visits from wealthy ladies and gentlemen of London society who were curious to see him. He died at the hospital on 11 April 1890, aged just twenty-seven. The official cause of death was asphyxia, although Treves, who dissected his body, said that Merrick died from a dislocated neck.

AT THE 250TH ANNIVERSARY the then London Hospital became the Royal London Hospital. Today the Royal London is part of Barts Health NHS Trust. The hospital specialises in tertiary care services for patients across London and elsewhere. The Royal London also provides general hospital services to the City and Tower Hamlets. Today much of the London Hospital is hidden by blue screens as redevelopment continues. Phase one opened on 1 March 2012 and saw 110 wards and departments with ill-configured facilities dating back to the eighteenth century moved into new state-of-the-art facilities. The second phase is now underway and is planned for completion in 2014. There are two parts to this second phase: firstly, to refurbish the Alexandra wing of the hospital and, secondly, to remove old hospital buildings and extend the north entrance to the new hospital.

HUGHES MANSIONS, VALLANCE ROAD

HUGHES MANSIONS, VALLANCE ROAD, 1929. Vallance Road was formerly
Baker's Row which was named after the late nineteenth-century clerk of
the Whitechapel Union, who was responsible for the Workhouse Infirmary.
Hughes Mansions were built in 1928 by B.J. Belsher, Borough Architect, and
this picture was no doubt taken to commemorate the then-new structures.
Hughes Mansion's was named after the famous author of *Tom Brown's
Schooldays*, who was also the father of Mary Hughes (1860–1941), a
voluntary parish worker. In 1928 Mary Hughes moved to no. 71a Vallance
Road next door to the pub that she converted into the Dewdrop Inn. The inn
was to act as a social centre and refuge for the local homeless. The Hughes
Mansions scheme consisted of three blocks and comprised 92 flats capable
of accommodating 462 people. The scheme covered an area of 1.3 acres and
its distinguishing features were an infant welfare centre and several lock-up
shops on the Vallance Road frontage.

THE LAST BOMB TO FALL on London fell on Tuesday 27 March 1945 – it was a V2 bomb which struck Hughes Mansions. Two of the three blocks of council flats were destroyed and 134 people were killed. In the post-war era, the council proposed to rebuild the blocks and improve the amenities of the estate. Additional lands were purchased in order to reduce the density of dwellings per acre, although the part of Hughes Mansion that was destroyed was not rebuilt. The site remains undeveloped and is now a children's playground and there is also a memorial plaque to those killed in the raid of 1945.

BOMB DAMAGE IN HANBURY STREET AND SPITAL STREET

BOMB DAMAGE IN HANBURY STREET and Spital Street to the north-west of the borough, September 1940. Between 7 September 1940 and 10 May 1941 London suffered 57 nights of bombing. Stepney was a key area for bombing raids because of the docks and its close proximity to the City. In aiming for the City of London much widespread destruction of the neighbouring borough occurred, which caused chaos for the residents. An example of the mass destruction can be seen in this picture, when Stepney was described as 'a vista of gashed streets, with the ambulances slowly moving and Air Raid Precautions (ARP) men frantically digging like dusty little terriers'. With buildings being razed to the ground, residents had to make alternative arrangements for shelter. Many left the area, but for those remaining many would retreat into the Underground stations. It was actually down to Communist leader Phil Piratin and the Stepney Tenants Defence League that the Underground stations of London were opened up for people to shelter in.

TODAY, HANBURY STREET and Spital Street are undergoing more modernisation. The building currently being constructed will be commercial premises on the ground floor with fourteen luxury flats on three floors above.

THE OLD TRUMAN BREWERY

THE BREWERY, BRICK LANE, Spitalfields 1842. The Truman Brewery is the former Black Eagle Brewery complex which was established by the brewers Truman and subsequently became Truman, Hanbury & Buxton. The site's first association with brewing is recorded in 1666 when Joseph Truman joined William Bucknall's Brewhouse in Brick Lane. Subsequently Truman became manager in 1697, and through his family's efforts, especially those of Sir Benjamin Truman, the brewery expanded rapidly over the next 200 years. By the mid-eighteenth century a new beverage flavoured with hops was introduced by the Huguenot immigrants, which became very popular. Truman initially imported hops from Belgium, but farmers in Kent soon began to grow hops to help meet the growing demand. In 1789 the brewery was taken over by Sampson Hanbury, and the Truman family became sleeping partners. In 1808, Thomas Fowell Buxton, Hanbury's nephew, joined the company. He improved the brewing process by converting to steam power and with the rapid expansion of the country's road and railway networks the brewery became famous across Britain.

BY 1835, TRUMAN WAS PRODUCING some 200,000 barrels of porter, a dark style of beer originating in London, per year. They faced competition from outside London, most notably Burton upon Trent where the water was particularly suitable for brewing, so by 1873 the company had acquired a brewery in Burton and began to build a new site named after the original Black Eagle Brewery. In 1888 Truman, Hanbury & Buxton became a public company with shareholders, but it was their premises in Burton that saw the main activity. The Brick Lane brewery was taken over by the Grand Metropolitan Group in 1971, followed in 1972 by a merger with Watney Mann. However, by this time the brewery was in a terminal decline and was to close in 1988. Today, the Old Truman Brewery has become a microcosm attracting many visitors. The former brewery buildings, warehouses and yards were redeveloped by the Zelof Partnership and are now a mixture of business and leisure blended together on the 11-acre site. The area houses over 250 businesses which include bars, restaurants, shops, creative businesses, events spaces, offices, workshops and weekly fashion markets.

BRICK LANE

BRICK LANE, 1935. The building on the left-hand side of the picture was first established in 1743 as a Protestant chapel by London's French Huguenot community. The Huguenots were refugees who had fled France to escape persecution from the Catholics. In 1809 the building became a Wesleyan chapel, but this was to only last a decade as by 1819 it had been taken over by the Methodists. In the late nineteenth century there was an influx of a new community, the Jewish from Russia and Central Europe, and the building became the Machzikei Hadas or Spitalfields Great Synagogue. Brick Lane was to become a centre for weaving, tailoring and the clothing industry due to the abundance of semi-skilled and unskilled labour.

TODAY WITH A LARGE BANGLADESHI COMMUNITY in the area, the building on the left is now a mosque called the Brick Lane Jamme Masjid or Brick Lane Great Mosque. The mosque can hold up to 3,000 people and is particularly crowded on a Friday during Jummah prayers. The building has been a mosque since 1976 and Brick Lane today is renowned for its Anglo-Indian cuisine. Cinnamon Brick Lane Restaurant has won the British Curry Club Award – Best in Brick Lane 2012.

WENTWORTH STREET

WENTWORTH STREET, c. 1900. Wentworth Street was an important thoroughfare, running from Brick Lane in the east to Middlesex Street in the west. The street was named after Thomas Wentworth, Earl of Cleveland, who owned much land in the area during the 1630s and '40s. By the nineteenth century much of the street had fallen on hard times, even though it was part of the thriving Petticoat Lane Market. The western half of the street was notable for its Jewish inhabitants in the late nineteenth and early twentieth centuries. However, the eastern half was of poorer character and was part of the slum district, defined by places such as George Yard, George Street and Thrawl Street, where the Charlotte de Rothschild Buildings were erected.

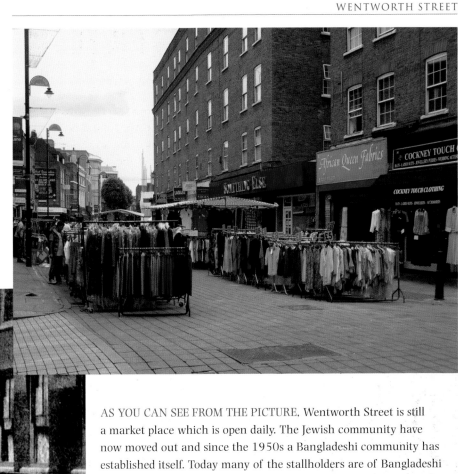

AS YOU CAN SEE FROM THE PICTURE, Wentworth Street is still a market place which is open daily. The Jewish community have now moved out and since the 1950s a Bangladeshi community has established itself. Today many of the stallholders are of Bangladeshi origin and they specialise in clothing, as do a lot of the shops in the vicinity, which reflects the traditional trade of the area.

CHARLOTTE DE ROTHSCHILD BUILDINGS

CHARLOTTE DE ROTHSCHILD BUILDINGS, Thrawl Street, between Commercial Street to the west and Brick Lane to the east, *c.* 1902. At the end of the nineteenth century Stepney was an overcrowded and unsanitary area and this was in part due to the significant number of poor Jewish immigrants ending up in the East End. The question of how to house this large population occupied parliament as well as the established Jewish bourgeoisie. The answer was classically Victorian: philanthropy, but philanthropy with a guarantee for the philanthropists. The Four Per Cent Industrial Dwelling Company Limited was founded by Nathan Mayer Rothschild in 1885 and aimed to provide 'the industrial classes with commodious and healthy Dwellings at a minimum rent'. The funds to build the dwellings were raised by issuing shares to investors who were guaranteed a four per cent return. The Charlotte de Rothschild Buildings were approved in 1886 and designed by N.S. Joseph. The dwellings were two parallel blocks, six storeys high above a semi-basement. The fronts are yellow brick gashed at intervals by the tall vertical openings that give light and air to the staircases. Two courses of red brick are used to give the effect of impost bands between the windows. Decoration was minimal with iron railings on the staircase landings.

TODAY THE ONLY PART of the building still in existence is the entrance archway. Between 1973 and 1980 the buildings were demolished and replaced with modern housing. Thrawl Street itself is a winding road that curves around the Flower and Dean Estate which was built between 1982 and 1984. Where Flower and Dean Walk emerges onto Wentworth Street is where the archway is positioned today.

THE JEWISH SOUP KITCHEN

THE JEWISH SOUP KITCHEN, Brune Street, 1967. The kitchen was originally opened in 1854 in Leman Street. It was relocated to Butler Street (now Brune Street) in 1902 and was financed by wealthier Jewish people. The ornate façade testified to the wealth of some sections of the Jewish community and was designed to offer inspiration to their less fortunate co-religionists. After the assassination of Tsar Alexander II in 1881 and the resulting pogroms, there was a huge influx of Jewish people, who often intended to go to America. However, many stayed in this country and in particular in the Spitalfields area due to its reputation as an area for cheap living and because many Jewish people had settled here before. By 1900, 95 per cent of the population was Jewish. The richer members of the community helped the poorer with the provision of food on Monday, Tuesday, Wednesday and Thursday of each week. The food consisted of either soup and bread or kosher margarine and sardines. On Thursdays pilchards and extra bread were given out to help the poor over the weekend. During the winter of 1931 over 4,000 people were seen nightly.

TODAY THE SOUP KITCHEN has gone, but the striking façade still remains. For many years the building stood empty, as a ghostly shadow, quietly reminding passers-by of the earlier residents of Spitalfields. However, in the late 1990s a commercial developer realised the potential of the Soup Kitchen with the building's close proximity to the City and elegant façade which could provide a prime location for exclusive flats. Thus this building has served new purposes, for investors seeking development sites in and around the City but also for City workers requiring accommodation within easy reach of their work. Whether this will help to regenerate the area in the long term is dependent on the extent to which the affluence of these new residents can be shared with the existing community.

LAMB STREET

LAMB STREET, SPITALFIELDS MARKET, *c.* 1912. The view on Lamb Street is looking at Spitalfields Market and east towards Commercial Street. Charles I gave a licence in 1638 for a market to sell flesh, fowl and roots on the site, which was then a rural area to the east of London. However, after a lapse in the market it was refounded in 1692 by Charles II. Over the next 200 years the market continued to do its best to provide fresh fruit and vegetables for the ever-expanding population. In 1876, former market porter Robert Horner purchased a short lease on the market and started work on a new market building which was completed in 1893 at a cost of £80,000.

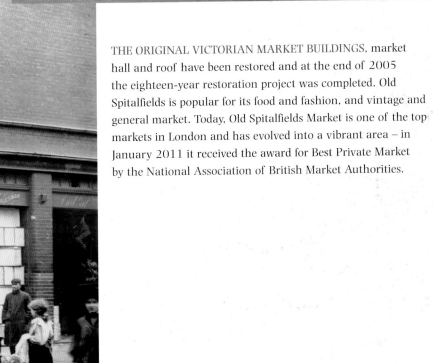

THE ORIGINAL VICTORIAN MARKET BUILDINGS, market hall and roof have been restored and at the end of 2005 the eighteen-year restoration project was completed. Old Spitalfields is popular for its food and fashion, and vintage and general market. Today, Old Spitalfields Market is one of the top markets in London and has evolved into a vibrant area – in January 2011 it received the award for Best Private Market by the National Association of British Market Authorities.

WHITECHAPEL ROAD

WHITECHAPEL ROAD, *c.* 1901. This picture of Whitechapel Road shows the Whitechapel Art Gallery and, next door to it, the Passmore Edwards Library. This picture may have been taken to commemorate the opening of the art gallery, as it was opened in 1901 by Lord Rosebery. Designed by Charles Harrison Townsend, it was the first publicly funded gallery for contemporary exhibitions in London. The gallery was the dream of the Revd Samuel Barnett of St Jude's Church, Commercial Street, and his wife Henrietta. As early as the 1880s the Revd Barnett had brought art to the East End by staging art exhibitions in a local school. In 1899 he began a charity to raise funds in order to build a permanent art gallery near the Whitechapel Library. Passmore Edwards was a lifelong champion of the working classes and was a generous benefactor and over a period of fourteen years, seventy buildings were established as a direct result of his bequests, the gallery and library on Whitechapel Road being beneficiaries. Outside the library is an obelisk which was erected in 1853. It had been an exhibit at the Crystal Palace in 1851 and was purchased by the Trustees of St Mary's, Whitechapel, to be used as a refuge for those crossing the wide and busy high street.

TODAY, THE OBELISK HAS GONE. It was removed in 1925 when the road was raised. The Passmore Edwards Library now provides an entrance to Aldgate East Underground station. To the east side of the station entrance is a blue plaque commemorating the poet and painter, Isaac Rosenberg, who lived in the East End and studied at the library. In 2005 the Whitechapel Art Gallery received a huge £3.26 million injection from the Heritage Lottery Fund, allowing the gallery to expand next door as the library has moved premises. On 4 April 2009 the gallery reopened after the two-year project was completed and in all the work cost £13.5 million. A new archive gallery, reading room, and an archive repository have all been created. These developments are all in keeping with the gallery's ethos as an educational charity.

WHITECHAPEL HAYMARKET

WHITECHAPEL HAYMARKET, LOOKING EAST along Whitechapel Road, *c.* 1926. The charter for the haymarket, which was to be held three times a week, was first given in 1708. To the east of the picture, one can see the spire of the St Mary Matfelon Church. Created as a chapel-of-ease and built in the fourteenth century, it is the second oldest church in the borough, with St Dunstan's being the earliest. Locally the church was known as the 'white chapel' because a mixture of chalk and lime was used to paint the outside of the original building, which gave it a bright white finish. The prominent position of the church on the westerly junction of the Whitechapel Road made it a landmark and thus gave the area its name. In 1673 the parish of Stepney was divided into nine separate parishes, and one of them was the parish of St Mary's, Whitechapel. The church ceased to be a chapel-of-ease and was dedicated to St Mary Matfelon. By now the original church was in a ruinous condition and in the nineteenth century a new church was built, which was opened and reconsecrated on 2 February 1877. However, three years after its opening on 26 August 1880 the building was destroyed by fire. The church was rebuilt and opened once more on 1 December 1882 with capacity for 1,600 worshippers.

TODAY, THERE IS NO SIGN of the Haymarket as it was abolished in 1929 due to the traffic congestion it caused. There is also no evidence of the spire of St Mary Matfelon as, on 29 December 1940, enemy fire destroyed the church. It was left in disrepair until 1952 before finally being demolished. The site of the church is now a public park called Altab Ali Park, and all that remains of the original building is a footprint outline.

STEPNEY COAT OF ARMS

UPON THE CREATION OF STEPNEY BOROUGH in 1899, a borough seal was adopted. The seal depicted the patron saints of the borough: St Anne, St George, St Dunstan and St Mary Matfelon. Also depicted was the Tower of London, a sailing ship and the quayside. However the seal was replaced by a coat of arms in 1931, as seen below, left. The main item on the shield is a ship and at the top the crossed anchors, all representing the strong maritime ties of the borough. The cross of St George is flanked on each side by a blacksmith's tongs to represent the patron saint of Stepney, St Dunstan. The soldier's helmet with the crown is to represent the Tower of London. Finally, the motto for Stepney adorns the bottom of the coat of arms: a *Magnis ad Maiora*.

THE TOWER HAMLETS COAT OF ARMS, St George's Pool, on the north side of The Highway. In 1965 the borough of Stepney was amalgamated with Bethnal Green and Poplar to form the new borough of Tower Hamlets and a new coat of arms was created. Much of Stepney's coat of arms was incorporated. The Latin motto *a Magnis ad Maiora* still remains, just in its English translation of *From Great things to Greater*. On the dexter side of the shield is a seahorse, again to represent the maritime roots of the borough. The sinister supporter is a Talbot dog, to represent the Isle of Dogs, another major part of the borough. Next to the tongs, in the middle, is a sprig of mulberry, which represents the silk industry, mulberry trees being the food for silk worms. To the right is a shuttle, for the weaving that used to take place. Finally, the White Tower is depicted at the top, as the Tower gives its name to the borough.